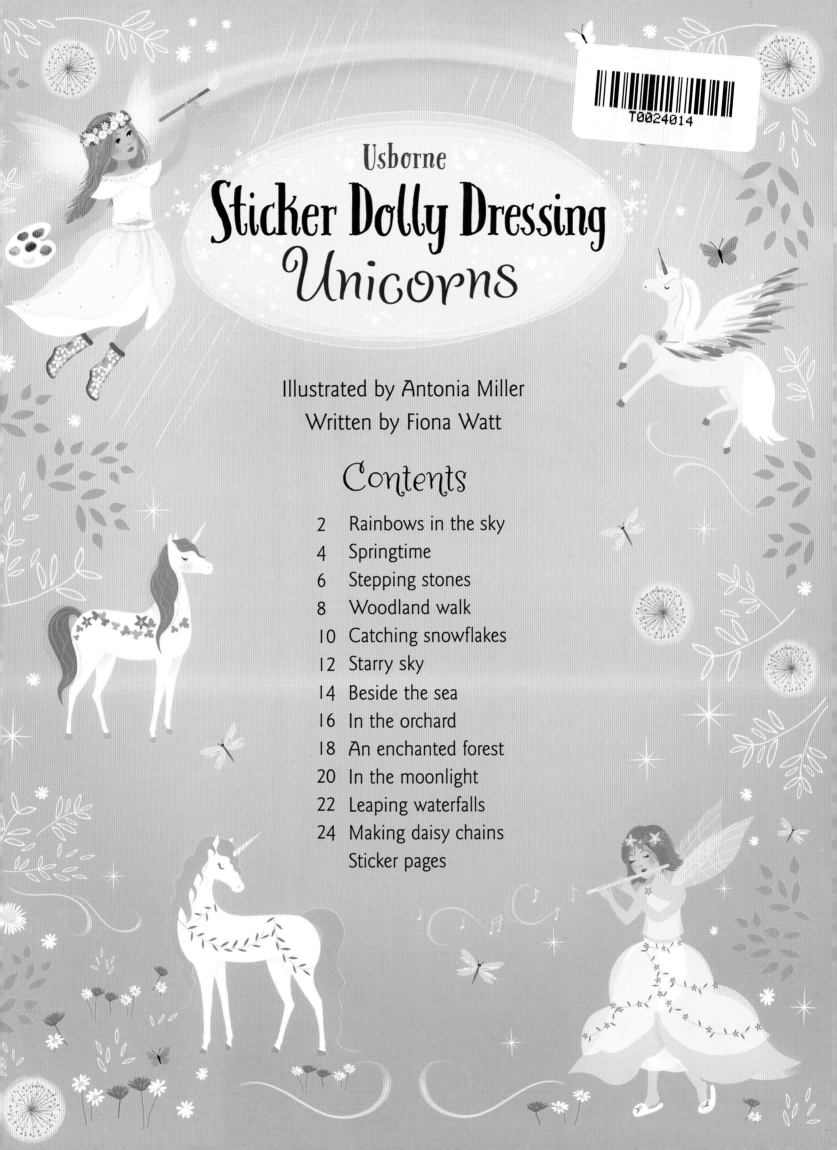

Usborne
Sticker Dolly Dressing
Unicorns

Illustrated by Antonia Miller

Written by Fiona Watt

Contents

T0024014

Rainbows in the sky

When the sun is shining brightly, but raindrops begin
to fall, Violet and Rosa paint rainbows across the sky.
Unicorns usually appear and soar gracefully around them.

Violet

2

Rosa

Springtime

As the cold sleepy months of winter drift away and the days become warmer, springtime buds burst into flower. Flora and Hester love wandering with their unicorns to watch the bees and butterflies that appear in search of sweet-smelling pollen and nectar.

Celandine

Flora

Hester

Columbine

Stepping stones

Mimosa and Clover tiptoe daintily across stepping stones at the edge of a pond to play with Moonflower and her foal, Rosehip. Clover throws bubbles into the air for Rosehip to burst on the tip of her horn.

Moonflower

Rosehip

Mimosa

Clover

Woodland walk

Princess Cora and Princess Faye live in a magnificent palace with their parents, the king and queen. Every afternoon they collect their unicorns from the royal stables and take them for a walk in the shady woodlands that surround the palace.

Cora

Sorrel

Faye

Willow

9

Catching snowflakes

When snow tumbles silently from the icy sky, Crystal and Avaline fly high above the snowy ground to try to catch as many snowflakes as they can. They're joined by flying unicorns that prance and flutter around them.

Crystal

Avaline

Starry sky

When the sky is illuminated with dancing purple and green lights, Luna and Aurora leap onto their unicorns and ride up into the stars. Shimmering fairy dust flows from their wands as they cast magical wishes for sleeping children everywhere.

Luna

Astra

Aurora

Starlight

Beside the sea

Unicorns and mermaids love to dive into the sea and play together in the gentle waves. Other sea creatures often hear the sound of the mermaids' laughter and come to join in the fun.

Marina

Oriana

Meriel

Fontana

In the orchard

Sunbeam and her foal, Twinkle, are dozing in the dappled shade beneath the branches of an old apple tree. Pippin and Dewberry are picking fruit from the tree, but Ambrosia is worried that they might disturb the sleepy unicorns.

Pippin

Sunbeam

Dewberry

Ambrosia

An enchanted forest

In a clearing in a forest, delicate notes flow from
Melody's flute and dance between the lantern-lit trees.
Unicorns, entranced by the beautiful music, stand
silently in the shadows, while glowing fireflies
flutter around in the cool night air.

Skylark

Moonbeam

Melody

In the moonlight

Every evening, if the night sky is clear, Queen Marilla leaves her palace and strolls around the royal estate to look at the moon and the twinkling stars. Caspian, her trusty unicorn, always trots silently beside her and leads her safely through the darkness.

Caspian

Leaping waterfalls

Unicorns leap through the cool water that cascades down a magnificent waterfall. When they are tired they climb out of the water to dry their wings, before flying off to play again.

Sweetpea

Stitchwort

Briar

Serena

Making daisy chains

In a sunny clearing at the edge of a forest, Kitty sits making delicate garlands from daisies that she has gathered. She'll make one for herself and some for Larkspur to wear on his head and around his neck.

Larkspur

Rainbows in the sky

Pages 2-3

Violet's outfit

Flowers for
Violet's hair

Wings
for the
unicorns

Put the
aprons on
after the tops
and skirts.

Rosa's outfit and
flowers for her hair

Springtime
Pages 4-5

Flowers for
Celandine's mane

A garland for
Columbine's back

Columbine's bell

Flowers for
Flora's hair

A bell for
Celandine's
neck

Put Flora's
skirt on
before her top.

Hester's
outfit

Clover's outfit and
flowers for her hair

Flowers for
Moonflower's
mane and back

Mimosa's
outfit

Garlands for Rosehip's
back and neck

Woodland walk

Pages 8-9

Put this halter around Sorrel's neck.

Sorrel's saddle

Put Cora's skirt on before her top.

Faye's outfit

Willow's halter and saddle

Catching snowflakes
Pages 10-11

Put the fairy dolls' skirts on before their jackets.

Crystal's jacket

Avaline's earmuffs and jacket

Crystal's skirt and boots

Avaline's skirt

Starry sky
Pages 12-13

Put Luna's skirt on before her top.

Aurora's outfit

Flowers for Starlight's mane

Beside the sea
Pages 14-15

Oriana's outfit

Marina's top

Fontana's halter and mane

Meriel's top and tail

A starfish for Meriel's hair

In the orchard

Flowers for
Pippin's hair

Twinkle

Dewberry's
outfit

Pippin's top
and skirt

Berries for
Sunbeam's
head

Flowers for
Ambrosia's hair

Ambrosia's
top and skirt

An enchanted forest
Pages 18-19

Windows for
the treehouse

The front door

Flowers for
Moonbeam's
back

A garland
for Skylark's
back

Flowers for
Melody's hair

Melody's
skirt

The tip of Marilla's staff

Caspian's crown

Marilla's crown

A garland for Caspian's neck

Put Marilla's skirt on first.

Leaping waterfalls

Pages 22-23

Flowers for
Stitchwort's head

A garland for
Briar's head

Stitchwort's
saddle

Sweetpea's
outfit

Serena's
boots

Serena's
outfit

Sweetpea's
boots

Making daisy chains

Page 24

Kitty's
outfit

Flowers for Larkspur's
head and neck